Helpers in my community

Bobbie Kalman

 Crabtree Publishing Company

www.crabtreebooks.com

Created by Bobbie Kalman

Author and Editor-in-Chief
Bobbie Kalman

Educational consultants
Reagan Miller
Elaine Hurst
Joan King

Editors
Joan King
Reagan Miller
Kathy Middleton

Proofreader
Crystal Sikkens

Photo research
Bobbie Kalman

Design
Bobbie Kalman
Katherine Berti

Production coordinator
Katherine Berti

Prepress technician
Katherine Berti

Photographs
American Red Cross: Talia Frenkel: p. 22 (bottom), 24 (bottom right)
Digital Stock: p. 20 (bottom), 21
Digital Vision: p. 8, 24 (top middle)
iStockphoto: p. 23 (top)
Shutterstock: cover, p. 1, 3, 4, 5, 6, 7, 9, 10, 11, 12,
     13, 14, 15, 16, 17, 18, 19, 20 (top), 23 (bottom),
     24 (except bottom right and top middle)

Library and Archives Canada Cataloguing in Publication

Kalman, Bobbie, 1947-
    Helpers in my community / Bobbie Kalman.

(My world)
Includes index.
ISBN 978-0-7787-9444-8 (bound).--ISBN 978-0-7787-9488-2 (pbk.)

    1. Community life--Juvenile literature. 2. Professions--Juvenile
literature. I. Title. II. Series: My world (St. Catharines, Ont.)

HM756.K34 2010   j307   C2009-906100-7

Library of Congress Cataloging-in-Publication Data

Kalman, Bobbie.
    Helpers in my community / Bobbie Kalman.
        p. cm. -- (My world)
    Includes index.
    ISBN 978-0-7787-9488-2 (pbk.) -- ISBN 978-0-7787-9444-8
(reinforced library binding)
    1. Community life--Juvenile literature. 2. Community workers--
Juvenile literature. I. Title. II. Series.

HM716.K35 2010
307--dc22
                                    2009041217

Crabtree Publishing Company

Printed in the U.S.A./022018/CG20180103

www.crabtreebooks.com   1-800-387-7650

Published in Canada
Crabtree Publishing
616 Welland Ave.
St. Catharines, Ontario
L2M 5V6

Published in the United States
Crabtree Publishing
PMB 59051
350 Fifth Avenue, 59th Floor
New York, New York 10118

Published in the United Kingdom
Crabtree Publishing
Maritime House
Basin Road North, Hove
BN41 1WR

Published in Australia
Crabtree Publishing
3 Charles Street
Coburg North
VIC, 3058

What is in this book?

What is a community?

A **community** is a place where many people live and work together.
Community helpers are people who make communities cleaner, safer, and better.
Who are the helpers in your community?

Some community helpers are builders,
doctors, teachers, and librarians.
All these people help you.

Buildings and roads

Communities need **buildings** where people can live or work. **Builders** build houses, offices, schools, and stores. They also build roads and bridges.

Builders use
these machines
to do their work.

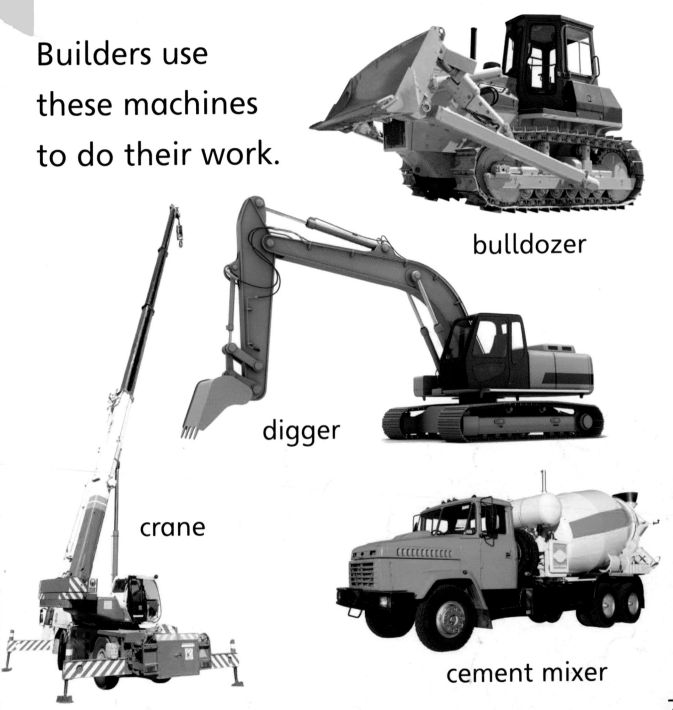

bulldozer

digger

crane

cement mixer

Electricity and water

People in a community need **electricity**. Lights, computers, television sets, and many other things cannot work without it. **Electricians** are people who make sure that communities have the electricity they need.

People need clean water in their homes. They drink water and use it to have baths and to wash their clothes.

Plumbers are community helpers who put in the pipes that carry the water to our homes.

Teachers and librarians

Teachers make learning fun and exciting. They teach us how to read and write. They teach us math, science, and social studies.

Librarians help us find the books we need.

Some librarians work in schools.

Some librarians work in community **libraries**.

Other school helpers

Some children walk to school. **Crossing guards** make sure the children cross the roads safely. **School-bus drivers** drive some children from home to school.

School **nurses** take care of children who are sick at school.

Principals make sure that everyone follows the school rules.

Caretakers clean schools and fix things.

Who are your school helpers?

school nurse

principal

Medical helpers

Medical helpers are doctors, nurses, and other people who keep us healthy. Some medical helpers work in offices. Others work in hospitals.

Dentists are doctors who care for our teeth.

They check our teeth and fix them.

They teach us how to have healthy mouths.

Emergency helpers

Emergencies are dangerous things that happen suddenly. **Emergency workers** help find people and take them away from danger.

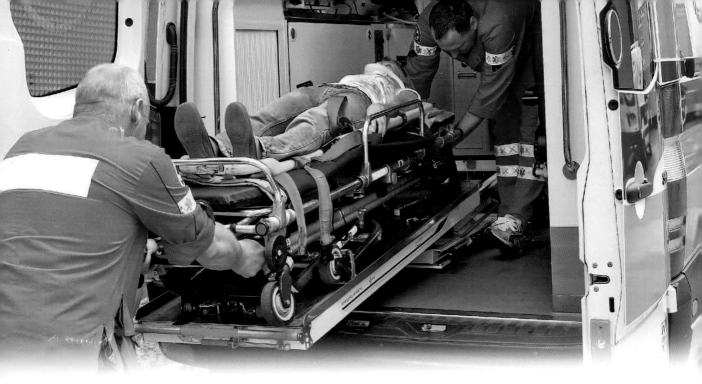

Paramedics bring sick or hurt people to hospitals. They take them to hospitals quickly in **ambulances**. They care for the people until they arrive at a hospital.

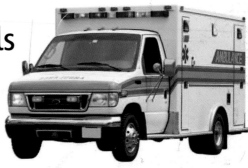
ambulance

Firefighters

Firefighters fight fires in buildings.

They also fight forest fires.

They rescue people and animals.

They risk their lives to help others.

Firefighters drive big trucks to fires.

fire truck

Police officers

Police officers protect people in their communities.
They make sure that people do not break the law.
They help people who are in trouble.

Police officers talk to children about
how to be safe in their communities.

Kind helpers

Volunteers are kind people
who help other people.
They do not get paid for their work,
but their jobs are very important!

You can be a volunteer, too.
You can help the Earth
by planting trees or
picking up trash.
How else could you help?

Words to know and Index

builders
pages
5, 6–7

electricians
page 8

emergency
helpers
pages 16–17

firefighters
pages
18–19

medical helpers
pages 5, 13, 14–15

plumbers
page 9

police officers
pages 20–21

school helpers
pages 5, 10–11,
12–13

volunteers
pages 22–23